Race Against Time

Written by William O'Byrne

Rigby

Race Against Time

Chapter Snapshots . . .

1. A Race Not To Be Missed

It's not just the runners who are waiting anxiously for the race to begin. People working for newspapers, radio, and television are ready to catch every second of the action.

2. They're Off!

The race has begun. Behind the scenes, in TV studios, radio stations, and newspaper offices, many people are also racing against time!

"The final of the 100

3. A Picture Is Worth A Thousand Words

Photographers have only a few seconds to capture great moments of the race action on film.

4. From The Stadium To The World

The race is over and the winner is celebrating. However, the newspaper, TV, and radio reporters are still working hard to spread news of the race to the world!

neter race is about to be run."

1. A Race Not To Be Missed

2:00

It is the Olympic Games. The final of the 100-meter race is about to be run. The crowd is cheering and clapping. There is an air of excitement within the stadium.

Athens

Where Did The Olympic Games Start?

The first Olympic Games were held in Olympia, Greece, in 776 B.C. Events at the early Olympic Games included track and field, boxing, wrestling, and horse racing. These Olympic Games were held every four years for more than 1,000 years.

The modern Olympic Games began in 1896 in Athens, Greece. At those Olympic Games, 14 countries competed in nine different sports. Today, almost 200 countries compete in more than 30 sports!

All around the world, people are waiting anxiously to see who will win the precious gold medal. Will it be the runner from the United States? The runner from Australia or the one from South Africa?

Trackside, 2:05 P.M.

2:05

The runners are lined up, ready to go. Their hearts are pounding. They are concentrating on the race ahead. Their muscles are warmed up and ready for action.

Newspaper Reporters' Room, 2:05 P.M.

Newspapers from around the world are eager to obtain interesting stories about what is happening at the games. They need to be able to tell people, through exciting writing and photographs, about all the action that is taking place.

News organizations from different countries know that their readers and listeners will mostly want to know about their own country's Olympic teams. Reporters check the medal tally each day to see whether their athletes have won bronze, silver, or gold medals.

Newspaper Facts

Newspapers were started in the time of the Roman emperor Julius Caesar more than 2,000 years ago. In those days, each copy of a newspaper had to be written by hand!

Today, the biggest selling newspaper in the world is a Japanese newspaper. It sells more than 10 million copies each day. It's a good thing we invented printing presses!

Newspaper reporters are writers that news-papers employ to uncover the best stories. Their job is to write articles that are interesting and accurate. At the Olympic Games, there are hundreds of newspaper  reporters, all trying to get first-rate stories. Their stories are written in many different languages, for many different readers, throughout the world.

A newspaper reporter must be able to write stories quickly and clearly. The time at which the story must be finished is called a deadline. If the reporter misses the deadline, the story has to wait for the following day's newspaper. By that time, it may be old news that no one wants to read.

Trackside, 2:05 P.M.

2:05

At the track, TV camera crews and reporters are making their final equipment checks. There is only one chance to report on each race, so they must not make any mistakes. Behind the TV cameras, there are many yards of cables that carry the pictures to studios in the stadium.

How Does A Television Work?

A television camera converts light into electrical energy, which is then sent to a transmitter. A transmitter changes the electrical energy into radio waves. The antenna connected to your television picks up the radio waves and turns them back into electrical energy. Your television changes the electrical energy into rays that shine onto your television screen to produce the picture. Your television produces 25 to 30 pictures every second!

Before the race, TV screens in the studio are tested to make sure everything works perfectly.

Television Broadcast Studio, 2:05 P.M.

Editors and directors in each TV studio choose the best scenes to show to their viewers. Often, they have to choose scenes immediately from many different cameras.

The History of Television

The first television was invented by a Scottish inventor named John Logie Baird. The first television broadcast was made in 1936. The first color television was invented in 1953.

How Does A Color Television Work?

On the screen of a color television, there are more than a million red, green, and blue dots. All the colors you can see on television are made by mixing up these dots, just like mixing up paints of different colors.

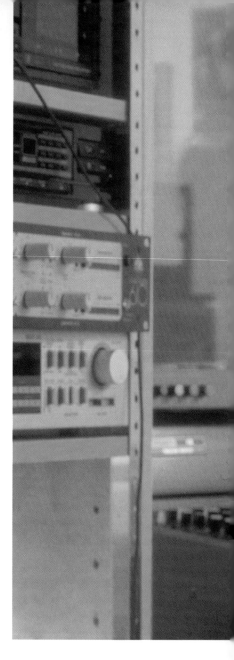

2:05

Radio Broadcast Studio, 2:05 P.M.

In another area of the stadium, people at radio broadcast studios are also busily preparing for the race. Radio announcers have been specially chosen for their ability to describe events quickly and accurately.

Because the radio listener cannot see what is happening, the announcer must be able to use interesting, descriptive language to help the listener imagine what is happening.

The announcer must also make the commentary exciting! If an announcer is good at his or her job, the listeners will feel as though they are actually seated in the stadium, watching the race.

2. They're Off!

Trackside, 2:10 P.M.

At last, we hear the starting gun. The race has begun! The athletes sprint at top speed to reach the finish line in the shortest time possible!

Race World Records

In running, a world record is the fastest official time that an athlete has ever been recorded running a race. World records can often change, as runners are always trying to run faster! Some of the fastest running times are given below:

Men:	100 meters	9.8 seconds
	200 meters	19.3 seconds
	400 meters	43.2 seconds
Women:	100 meters	10.4 seconds
	200 meters	21.3 seconds
	400 meters	47.6 seconds

As the TV news director watches the race live, he or she makes many decisions about which pictures of the race to show. The pictures change almost instantly. As the race is over in only 10 seconds, the director needs to be able to think and react very quickly.

The pictures that are chosen are sent instantly to a transmitter and, from there, to a satellite orbiting high above the earth.

From the satellite, the pictures are transmitted down to the TV station's receivers, and out to televisions around the country.

Because in a race there is no second chance, a television crew must make *no* mistakes.

13

2:18

Radio Broadcast Studio, 2:10 P.M.

While the race is being run, the radio announcer tells the listeners about the positions of the runners. They want to know who is in the lead. Where is the runner from our country? How is the crowd reacting? What does it feel like to watch the race? The announcer has a lot to describe in only 10 seconds!

Radio transmitter sends signal to satellite.

Satellite transmi

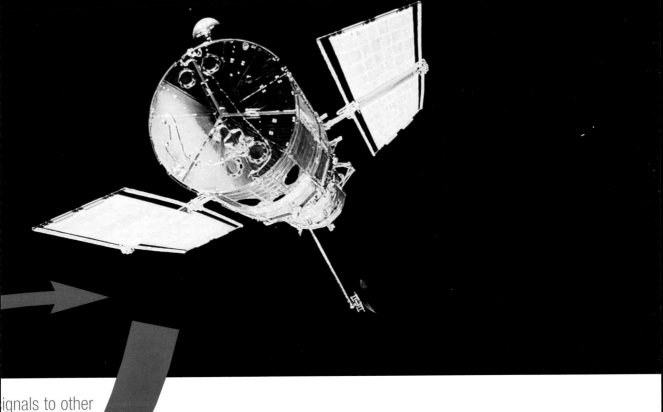

ignals to other
ountries.

The announcer speaks into a microphone connected to a radio transmitter. The radio transmitter sends a signal to a satellite orbiting the earth, and this signal is then transmitted to the announcer's radio station.

The radio station broadcasts the voice of the announcer to radios in the area. The announcer must be very careful not to say the wrong thing because thousands of people will hear!

15

3. A Picture Is Worth A Thousand Words

Newspaper Reporters' Room, 2:10 P.M.

To get their story to the newspaper quickly, reporters need to use fast technology. They may type their story into a laptop computer and use it to fax their story to the newspaper. They may e-mail their story from their computer to another one at the newspaper's offices. Both of these communication methods are very quick. As soon as the reporters write their story, they can send it immediately to the newspaper to meet their deadline.

The newspaper readers also want to see photographs of their favorite sports heroes in action.

A newspaper photographer is responsible for taking exciting action photographs. The reporter and the photographer work together to decide which photographs to send to the newspaper offices.

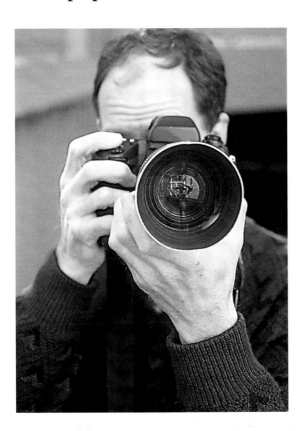

Timeline of Cameras

- Leonardo da Vinci invents a simple type of camera. — 1515

- A French doctor takes the world's first photograph. — 1826

- The world's first aerial photograph is taken from a balloon. — 1858

- A photograph appears in a newspaper for the first time. — 1880

- The first simple camera for personal use is invented. — 1889

- The world's first telephoto lens is invented. — 1891

- Astronauts take the first photographs of the moon. — 1969

- An electronic camera, which stores pictures on computer disk, is invented. — 1988

- A camera that uses CD-ROMS to store pictures is invented. — 1990

The photographer develops the photographs as quickly as possible. Often, photographs are scanned into computers and then sent by e-mail to the newspaper. Or they are transmitted by very high-quality fax machines designed especially for photographs.

Today, some photographers use digital cameras. Digital cameras use a computer disk instead of film, to store pictures. The pictures on the disk can be sent anywhere in the world quickly and easily by computer.

Newspaper Photographs

If you look closely at a newspaper photograph, you will see that it is made up of thousands of tiny dots. When we look at the dots from a distance, our eyes and our brain combine the dots to make a picture.

2:11

The race has just finished! The crowd is wildly excited! The winner runs a victory lap around the stadium!

A Story's Journey At The Newspaper

A story is written by the newspaper reporters.

The story is checked by the copy editors, ar photographs are chose by photo editors.

The managing editor decides where the story and the photographs will be placed in the newspaper.

The pages are made into film. The film is then used to make printing plates to print from.

Before the newspaper is printed, the first page proofs are checked.

Thousands of copies are printed.

Newspapers are delivered to homes, newsstands and stores all over the area.

4. From The Stadium To The World

Back at the newspaper office, a copy editor checks the reporter's story to make sure it reads well and that there are no spelling mistakes. The copy editor must be able to work quickly and accurately.

In another area of the newspaper office, a photo editor is looking over the photographs that have been received from the photographer.

The photo editor must select the best photograph to go with the story. The photograph must give the reader lots of information about the race—with plenty of eye-catching action.

Both the photo editor and the copy editor work with the newspaper's managing editor to decide where the story will appear. If it is an important story, it will appear on the front page. A front-page story has very important news, and often has eye-catching photographs. Different parts of the story may also appear in the sports section or the special Olympic Games section of the newspaper.

Trackside, 2:20 P.M.

After the race, radio announcers, newspaper reporters, and television reporters try to interview the winner as well as other athletes from their home countries. They will hurry down to the track to ask such questions as, "What did it feel like to win? How did you prepare for the race? Were you happy with the way you ran? What is your next event?"

What A Shot!

A great photo can capture all the excitement and emotion of a race. In this photo, the photographer manages to show exactly how Cathy Freeman felt after winning a silver medal in the 400-meter final at the Atlanta Olympics in 1996.

Everywhere around the world, people are interested in hearing or seeing how the athletes looked and felt after the race.

Around the world, 2:30 P.M.

In many countries around the world, television stations, newspapers, and radio stations are connected to the Internet. As news of the Olympic Games becomes available, a team of people collects the information, and types it into Web sites on the Internet. They may use photographs, video images or stories that they have received.

What Is The Internet?

The Internet is a collection of computers that are linked up all around the world. The Internet started in 1984, when many American universities linked up their computers. Today, millions of people in schools, homes, and offices are connected to the Internet.

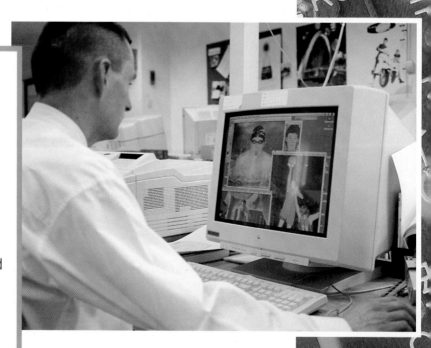

28

How Do Computers Communicate Over The Internet?

We can communicate with other computers over the Internet. Often, we use the Internet to send messages to other computer users. To send messages over the Internet, we need to use a modem. A modem changes the messages from our computers into signals that can be transmitted through the telephone system.

The computer operators enter the information and images onto their Web sites. Everywhere around the world, people with computers can log onto the Web sites of different news organizations and look at their reports. They can also visit other Web sites to find out specific information about a particular sport or athlete.

Around The World, 2:35 P.M.

By the time the medal ceremony is held, the newspaper office will have decided where they will put the story in the newspaper. The printing plates that are used to print the newspaper will have been made. The huge printing presses will have been started up to print the next day's newspaper.

The television stations may broadcast their pictures and the radio stations may repeat their commentaries throughout the day. Everyone will know who won the 100-meter finals race.

Newspaper Printing

A newspaper is printed on huge printing presses. In a printing press, ink is put onto parts of a metal plate that have pictures or words on them. When the metal plate is pressed onto a sheet of paper, the ink forms pictures and words on the paper.

Trackside, 2:45 P.M.

`2:45`

The next race has started. The next gold medal winner— who will it be?

Index

Race Against Time

More challenging sports action in these
Bookweb books!

Extreme Sports—Nonfiction

Technosports—Nonfiction

Capsize!—Fiction

Key To Bookweb
Fact Boxes

☐ **Arts**

☐ Health

☐ **Science**

☐ Social Studies

☐ Technology